T

Blueprint: Your Guide to Collegiate Success

Hulian Terrell

Table of Contents

Preface

Wait! As a student I know a lot of you are probably thinking about skipping this preface. I know that I used to. Before you go on to read this book, I just want to let you guys know how proud I am of you. Wherever you are in life I am proud and rooting for all of you, whether you are a student or just someone supporting me by reading this book. I believe that the beauty in life is in the journey more so than the destination. A lot of you are looking forward to beginning or graduating college, which is an awesome thing but remember, the lessons you learn and the experiences that you go through in school will follow you for as long as you live. Sometimes along our journey in life, we run into lessons disguised as bumps or learning curves. I have always been under the belief that these tough lessons should be shared for those who come after us. I have been fortunate enough to experience college and it has brought me so many opportunities and relationships. During my six years in and out of school, I was a Division 1 student athlete, a drop out, a transfer student, a resident assistant, a drop out a second time, a student worker, an intern, a boyfriend, an ex-boyfriend, and eventually I went on to graduate in the top 10% of my class (Shouts out to Purdue University Northwest!).

I had all of these experiences, but I also had to learn a lot of tough lessons that shaped me. After I graduated, I began to think of ways that I could give back. The conclusion I came to was to write a short book teaching students the correct ways to maneuver through college in order to avoid a few of the bumps and learning curves that I ran into. Other than a few personal stories that I share, this book gets right to the point and will be a quick and easy but very important read for you. I am no experienced author; I am merely a college graduate that is currently an operations manager in logistics. So with that being said, enough of my chatter. I want you guys to get on with this book because there is important information throughout that you will carry with you not only through college but through life. Congratulations on putting yourself in a position to better your life and partake in an experience that will grant you many memories and your own lessons. The only thing that I ask of you is to take any lessons that you learn from this book or in your own journey and pass them on to whoever comes after you. This is how we evolve and eventually make the world a better place. Happy reading.

Oh and one more thing, it is currently 2020 and I wrote this book during a national pandemic under quarantine. Always remember, good things can always come out of unfortunate situations. Never give up and never give in. Enjoy!

Chapter 1: Your Why

Why? Why is probably the most asked question in the history of the universe. Why is most likely the first question that you ever asked and quite frankly maybe the most frequent one that you'll use. There are also the questions "Who?" "What?" "When?" and "Where?," but without having a Why, these other questions are irrelevant. So why is "Why" so important, and why am I starting a book about college off with your why? It's simple. Why is the fuel that we use to do the things that we do. There has been nothing in the history of history that has been created or accomplished without a strong reason why. Throughout your time in life and especially in college, you will learn about and study people who went on to do great things that all stemmed from a reason that was greater than themselves. The reason that I titled this chapter "Your Why" is because it cannot be because someone else wants you to do it, it has to be something you want. "Why" is your fuel, you can only borrow someone else's fuel for so long before you burn out, which is why if you're in college to appease a parent or a loved one then congratulations you're here, but you will most likely not make it to the end. College is too much of a commitment to be there in order to appease someone else. If you're in this position right now, it is ok, but you should find out why you are there ASAP before things get difficult and you have to start your day at 8 a.m. with 3 or 4 back to back classes and then an 8-hour shift at work.

Do not confuse having a why with meaning knowing exactly what you want to do after college. You might not know where you want to end up after school, but you should know why you are using college to benefit your life later on. Do you want to be able to have a higher income? Are you here to eventually get into med or law school? College is merely a means to an end and should be treated as such and taken full advantage of. What do I mean by this? Throughout the years, college has been seen as less of a tool to further your life and more of a magic wand that will automatically grant you whatever it is that you want after you graduate. A lot of universities understand this, which is why tuition can sometimes be through the roof! They understand that some students are willing to take out a large amount of loans in order to be promised the life that they want afterwards. The biggest value that being in and graduating college gives you is access. It is basically just a tool or a key to open doors that others without degrees may not be able to open or will take a longer time to open. Although this may be the case you will end up with the same key to the same door to the same room that hundreds or even thousands of other students will get at the same time as you in the same place. How will you differentiate yourself? How will you use the access that college gives you to maximize your life for yourself and for your family? Throughout this book I am going to lay out a blueprint on how to achieve these things, but if your "why?" isn't big enough, you will struggle often and won't have enough fuel to see this thing through. In asking the question why, we reveal purpose or motive that will eventually be the rock we stand on when things start to get hard. Take some time out and really think about your "why?" and what it means to you. I promise you this will come in handy when the thought of quitting or walking away comes around. It will make quitting that much easier or that much harder for you when you understand your why and your purpose.

College comes with a lot of freedoms which is awesome, but freedom is maybe the biggest freshmen killer there is on campus. For those of you who have spent some time in college already, harken back to all of the freshmen that you came in with and how a lot of them lost focus and are no longer in school with you. (If you are one of those college dropouts I am speaking of, congratulations. Reading this book means that you are ready to turn things around and I am beyond proud of you). Think about how freedom took opportunity away from these people. In my opinion, the best way to teach discipline is to introduce freedom. Sounds like some sort or contradiction right? No way. In high school it was easier to be disciplined because there was so much structure and things that you had to do, or you'd be in trouble. I'm sure you've already heard that college is not like this at all. More freedom is to be had, more choices are to be given, and with these freedoms and choices, more discipline has to be exercised. This is why freedom and discipline go hand and hand. Lean too far one way and you will burn out but lean too far the other way and your life will lose structure and your life will unravel.

Discipline is never the sexiest of topics, but it will be the key ingredient of almost everything that you do and accomplish in college. Learning how to master yourself and college starts with discipline. Everyone's discipline looks different. A triathlete will have different standards and levels of discipline for themselves than say a competitive eater would. Based on how you live your life and the things that you want to accomplish, you will go about discipline in very different ways, but the thing that makes everyone's discipline the same are the non-negotiables. Let me let you in on a secret. A lot of individuals come up short with their discipline because they focus too much on what they want to do instead of what they don't want to do. Let me explain. Committing to run 4 miles, 4 times a week sounds a lot harder than committing to not being inactive and in the house 6 times out of the week. Running the 4 miles for 4 days may get you quick initial results but how long are you going to keep this up before you start negotiating with yourself about only running 3 miles the next time? Soon, you start feeling like your progress calls for you to be allowed to skip a day of running. Before you know it, you haven't ran in almost a month! Now imagine if you made a deal with yourself for it to be a non-negotiable to get out and be active for 6 days out of the week. For the first month you may just go on walks, but eventually you get bored with that and do some running. You may not get the quickest results but making things non-negotiable in your life promotes sustained discipline. It's almost like using a muscle over and over again. When going into your college schedule (which we will cover in the next chapter) make an agreement with yourself about the things that you won't allow. Don't go into the year with 4.0 goals and other difficult things to obtain that you historically have not. Begin with the things that you will not allow yourself to do and you will find things beginning to start working in your favor. Make it a non-negotiable to not skip class, make it a non-negotiable to not let any question that you have in class go unanswered. These are very simple things that will allow you to practice long-term discipline.

Have you ever heard someone say, "I wait until the last minute because I work better under pressure."? Never subscribe to this mindset. I used to do it all the time, when in reality I just didn't have enough self-discipline to get things done early, so I used the deadline to give me the motivation I needed to get the task done. This is a bad habit that builds strong reactionary tendencies. It will cause you to let life happen to you while you just simply react to whatever comes your way due to the lack of being a self-starter. This can eventually spiral into depression and feeling stuck.

I know that I must sound dramatic to some of you right now comparing procrastinating an assignment to depression, but this is very serious. Life does not care about your goals and desires. Family members will pass away unexpectedly, your car will start to break down on you while your money is low, or your girlfriend/boyfriend may break up with you out of the blue. These unfortunate scenarios are the reason that your discipline and your why must be strong. If you wait until the last minute to do work because it motivates you to finish, chances are high that you will begin to wait for other things to happen in life before you act. Life is awesome when you take advantage and take action instead of reaction.

Apologies! I know you guys aren't here to read or listen to me preach but before I go into the meat and potatoes of laying out this blueprint I wanted to make sure you guys are ready to receive this information. This short first chapter is only here to let you know that throughout college and life, your purpose and your discipline are tools that you will use to construct the blueprint that I am about to lay out for you. This book will be of little or no value to you don't have a strong reason for obtaining a degree and the discipline to accomplish the goal to get to your purpose. I am by no means the sharpest tool in the shed or the most gifted person in the room. I was simply a student like you are now, who made a number of mistakes and ran into countless roadblocks but still managed to maximize my opportunities and get the most out of my college career. I speak your language, and I am here to make sure you maximize your time in college even more than I did, over a shorter period of time, making fewer mistakes, and running into fewer roadblocks. That is my "why."

Welcome to *The College Blueprint*.

Chapter 2: Your Organization

When you hear the word organization in terms of schooling, you may think of folders, backpacks, pencil holders, or other things that may keep your life orderly or more easily accessible. When I talk about organization in terms of college, I mean looking at yourself as a business or an organization if you will. A key focus in almost every organization is efficiency. Efficiency is just another word for effectiveness. Every organization has different strengths that they play to in order to maximize their efficiency. Right now I want you to picture Target and Walmart. In the world of dying retailers, why do these two juggernauts continue to thrive? These places have a lot of similar items as well. Does this mean that they run their businesses the exact same to achieve the same success? Absolutely not! Walmart and Target could not be any more different yet they each share a big slice from the same pie. This is why in college you should run yourself as an organization instead of following what worked for someone else.

"But Hulian, why am I reading this book then?" Because I am not trying to give you cookie cutter ways that will give results to everyone, I am trying to give you the tools so that you can build your own success. Running yourself as an organization in college will allow you to take your strengths and leverage them to give you the ultimate return on your scholarly investment.

If I try to work in an environment that is too comfortable, clean, and orderly, then I will definitely fall asleep. I fell asleep maybe a dozen times alone while writing this book in the comfort of my home. While in undergrad, I always had to do my work in the library. I called my time in the library my office hours. It was something about the library that gave me the vibe that made me want to grind out whatever assignment I was facing or test I was studying for. I fed off of the energy from others and that helped keep me accountable and finish the task at hand. This worked for me and was a big reason I was able to be successful with schoolwork in my later years. For someone else, studying or doing homework in the library might sound like torture or a bunch of distraction. I have a friend who would go into the library with good intentions but leave with barely anything done because she spent most of her time people watching. An accessible work environment that is conducive to your focus and effectiveness (there's that "effective" word again), will be a necessity for you going forward. In college there will be a myriad of things going on daily and there will need to be a place where you can stop everything for a bit and unpack what went on that day or the day before, and what the forecast will look like for the next day. This place also needs to be somewhere where you can get work done with the most focus possible. As I've stated, I called this time my office hours and you should look into having this dedicated time too for at least three days a week. Doing this consistently throughout your time in college will help to ensure three key things.

1. You will almost never miss an assignment.
2. You will have actual free/relax time

3. You will have a grasp on even your most difficult class.

On the surface these three things might seem like common sense but allow me to go into detail on each point starting with the first. In college missed assignments are a norm. Missing assignments in college is so widespread that most professors offer partial credit for turning in things past their due date. If you're reading this book and have gone to, or are still in college, chances are high that you have not only missed an assignment, but you also found out that you missed it days after the assignment was due when you go to check your grades.

Why is it so easy to miss assignments? Well, have you ever signed up for a free trial of something and a month later you forgot about it and then it charged your credit card and you only find out once you go to check out your bank account? That's exactly what online assignments are like in college. Most of the time they are going to be due at the same time and on the same day on a weekly basis. If you have four classes with online assignments, you can quickly see how keeping up with everything can become a daunting task. Missing these assignments will eventually cause you to take a hit on your GPA.

If you have a dedicated time that you give to office hours, you can eliminate this problem because you have an assistant. You have an assistant that you will sit down and go over your current and next few days with. This assistant will be manual, and it is called your planner. No, your planner can't go get you a coffee or take your dog out for a walk like a normal assistant, but it will keep you on point just the same. There are many planners out there, you can choose to get as simple or as complex as you'd like. I always kept some sort of journal because writing things down rather than typing them always helped me to retain information a little longer. Every organization has an agenda or schedule of things that need to be followed for the day. Your world is no different. In the beginning of the year transfer all of your set dates into your planner. This includes everything on all of your syllabi, workdays, special events, anything that has a date that is dedicated should be written down before the end of the first week of classes. This is your schedule that you have to work around during the semester. This brings me to an important point, and that is that you should always make assignments in your planner due a day before the due date. If you're in a class that you can work ahead in, take advantage of that, but in most classes the professor will open up an assignment at the beginning of the week, and make it due at the end of the week. Most of the time students get done with these assignments' days before the due date but other times these assignments can be forgotten or done at the last minute. The best way that you can make sure that this never happens to you is to move these assignments a day ahead in your planner, this way that if it does slip your mind, your assistant has your back. Don't look at the early due date as a soft due date. If possible, please do every assignment at least one day before it is due. By doing this, you will not be working against the clock and you will have more clarity when doing the work. You can be the most forgetful human on earth but if you use your planner the way that I have outlined, you will be able to lean on it and not even bother remembering what and when was due. This brings me to my second point which is free time and relaxation.

Hear me out, I understand that a lot of you reading this right now have jobs (as you should, but we will get into that in another chapter) and finding time for yourself can be difficult. Some students have been able to get by going hard for four years nonstop, but none of their time belonged to themselves and they usually did not get the most out of their college experience. It is possible to work hard and have some time for yourself, but you have to demand it just like how your job and school demand time from you.

For some insight on this, I want you to take a look at someone who is really into fitness. These people are usually pretty disciplined but more importantly, a lot of them always seem to be in a good mood. Let them tell it and they will attribute exercise to making them feel good, but I want to dive a little deeper than that. Fitness enthusiasts and those alike have a hobby or lifestyle that requires a very structured way of living. A specific example that I want you to think about is the way that they go about food. A lot of these kinds of people meal prep. There are many reasons why they do this but a big thing that it does is save them time. In a time crunch, they can't go to McDonald's for a quick dollar menu item, but they also don't want to spend the time cooking or buying a usually more expensive option at a restaurant or fast food joint week in and week out. They get their cooking done early so that is one less issue that they have to deal with. They know what they are going to eat, when they are going to eat, when they are going to work out, what they are going to do during their workout, what time they look to go to sleep and how much sleep they will get. These individuals have a lot to do, but they knock out things like cooking early and live the rest or their lives on auto pilot because they structure their days as such. It is easier to be disciplined when you can see what it does for you and the time that it can save. Extra time is created more easily by structure. Having more extra time for yourself will allow you to perform maintenance and self-care. You will hear self-care being preached a lot in college. The term "burned out" will be associated with the lack of self-care. Burnout is a real thing, but it usually doesn't come in the form of a student just giving up or crashing like you may think. Your body is an amazing organism that always tries to adjust itself when something is off balance. Internally speaking, this is an amazing thing that helps you fight off sickness and disease. Externally speaking, it isn't always the best thing. The way burnout happens externally is that you will slowly start to neglect things that aren't mandatory in your life. You may become too tired to spend time with your family or go out with your significant other on a regular basis. Next chapter, we will discuss relationships and why they are such a vital part in your life in college. When the lack of self-care causes you to neglect your passions, relationships, or other things that do not require a mandatory time slot in your life, you will start to feel isolated. This is the first stage of burnout. Some people love isolation and it helps them work more effectively but working in isolation is different than isolating yourself because you are consumed by work. This will make you start to resent the mandatory work because you feel like it is affecting your relationships in a negative way. Consequently, just as your body balances itself out in sickness internally, externally you will begin to balance out your life by cutting out or neglecting the things that you feel are making you unhappy. This is the second and most visible stage of burnout that most of us recognize. Grades begin to drop, classes stop being attended to, performance at work takes a hit. Long story short, rest and self-care helps you to be more well-rounded in your work-relationship life. Ignoring yourself is playing yourself at the end of the day. Structuring your life so that you will have time for yourself is your responsibility.

Pro tip #1, never have too much on your plate because you will become fed up and end up throwing things away. You would rather be fully involved in three things, than to try and half-ass eight. Get into your scheduled office hours, and school is one less barrier that you will have when seeking personal time.

The third and final thing that I will touch on is the fact that structuring your time will give you a better grasp at those difficult classes. Listen, this is the College Blueprint. Your days of failing or having to retake classes are over after you apply the knowledge of this book because I am going to provide you with the recipe to never fail a class.

This recipe only has four steps. The first step is self-awareness. In college at least once or twice a semester you will experience a challenging course. Your most challenging course should NEVER be an elective. In the next chapter we will discuss how your guidance counselor can help you steer clear of those unwanted electives. After attending about a week of your classes, self-awareness will allow you to sit down and have an honest conversation with yourself about which classes will give you the most trouble. We all are different, and we have different learning styles, so a class that may be a breeze to you, may be a nightmare to a classmate of yours. Do not let your peers' opinion of am easy class that may be a challenging class for you cause you to think that there is something wrong with you. Have the awareness to recognize your hard class or classes and then you will be able to move on to the second step.

The second step is to determine the resources that will be available to you for help with this class. During my time in college I realized that there are so many free resources available to students that will help them flourish that are rarely used until times of desperation. People only want to run to the library or tutoring center when that final is coming up or a class might be failed. Why stress yourself out this way? Seek out the resources that will help you with the class and work that into your regular schedule. For me, I had a tight schedule as do most of us do but I had a calculus class that was a thorn in my side. I never had much patience with math and the professor had a heavy Russian accent that made it difficult to follow along. I knew that I would need outside help, so I turned to the free tutoring center. I only had time to go twice a week, but I went every single week. Even during the weeks that I think I didn't need help, I made sure I went at the same time on the same days because I knew that questions would arise when I started to study or do homework.

If no questions came to me then I would then venture to the third step which is reading ahead. In a good amount of your classes, your professor will or have already told you that you should read ahead before class. This information is *GOLD*, but a lot of your professors go about the wrong way of packaging it.

Do not read the whole chapter and try to understand everything. Read enough about the chapter so that you will have a general idea about what will take place next class. Most of you wouldn't go pay for a movie without at least seeing the trailer first and reading a little ahead is like the trailer to the next lesson that is ahead. Each chapter will usually begin with one to three ideas that will be used throughout the lesson. Some of it will be information that was used in previous chapters but there will always be a new idea touched on. Read about that new information and that will provide you with two opportunities to grasp the general idea of things. One opportunity by yourself, and the other with a professor that will be able to answer any questions.

Pro tip #2, if you want to know that you have a general understanding about what will be discussed in your next class, try doing the first one to three problems in the book (if your textbook has problems associated with it). In most textbooks these problems are located directly after the first section of each chapter, but some don't have any questions until the end of the whole chapter. You do not have to do this, but it will provide you with the confidence to go into the next class and feel like you can handle what is being thrown at you. It's like splashing yourself right before you jump into a cold pool. You get a chance to brace yourself.

The fourth and final step is to be completely focused and active in the classroom. In a challenging class, you cannot afford to miss a drop of information, so your distractions have to be at a minimum. Personally, I put my cell phone in my backpack so I wouldn't even feel it buzz and be tempted to look at it. If you have a child or children this obviously may not be an option, but all distractions have to be limited. The biggest distraction that I saw in undergrad were laptops. Yes people may have been online shopping or checking their social media feeds but that's usually only done in easier classes. The way that laptops distract people in harder classes is by allowing them to take down every single bit of information in class and be left with way too many notes. This makes things a nightmare when you go to study. Most professors will already have all of their power point slides available to you online, so you don't need to have every bit of information typed out. Writing down your notes allows you to jot down only the important bits of information. The idea is not to memorize the information provided to you, it's instead to understand it. This is why we teach kids exactly why 1 plus 1 equals 2. It is so that they can know why 2 plus 3 will equal 5. If they only memorized that 1 plus 1 equals 2 and 2 plus 3 equals 5, they would have a hard time figuring out other problems. This is why it seems like tests are unfair. Sometimes they don't have examples from the lessons that we covered in class. Professors want to test our understanding of information, not how well we memorize certain examples. That is why homework might look like 7+2 or 5+8 but the test looks like 13+25+6. If you only memorize *what* things are instead of understanding *why* things are, then you will always run into problems during tests.

If you are consistent with these four steps, then congratulations, failing a class is one less worry that you can check off your list of stress in college. Your simpler classes are like old cats in that you only really have to maintain them by providing basic needs. Difficult classes are like puppies and constantly need attention and work. Neither is more or less important than the other, one will just take more work to get those credits.

Living a life that includes structure takes work up front but having that structure and organization will reward you with so much more time and peace of mind. When you start to look at yourself as the organization or the business, it helps you realize how being efficient with your time helps you have more time to do the things that you want to do in life. As we become older, we start acquiring the means to do the things we want in life. Unfortunately, we also start to have less and less time to do these things. Declutter and organize the way you live so you will have more space to chase your dreams.

Chapter 3: Your Relationships and Resources

If you are a business student or have been around any type of business in some capacity, you may have heard of the word "leverage." In this sense, leverage is basically using resources that you already have, to help you gain something. For example, a kid might use her dad's old lawn mower to make extra money in order to buy a used car at the end of the summer. She effectively will use the lawn mower as leverage to purchase a car. Even if your college experience is strictly online, you should always be using resources that are available to you in order to make valuable gains. Right now, you are using this book as leverage to navigate effectively through college.

This book will save you a lot of time, effort, and some pain on your university journey. In college, leveraging your relationships and resources (or R&R as I like to call it) will be the key thing to do when attempting to separate yourself from the crowd. Your ability to network and gain valuable information or tools is a huge advantage that not everyone used while in school. If you are in college to just show up, go to class, and leave, you are going to miss out on so many opportunities that will later on open doors for yourself.

The Office of the Registrar

Let us begin with the first R in R&R which are your relationships with people. There are two types of relationships that you will cultivate in college, which are those of your professors and administration and then those of your peers. We will start with your relationships with your professors and administration. These are people who are employees and are paid to educate and help guide you on your journey through college. For many of you who are new to college or trying to find the right fit, the office of admissions will be your first point of contact. These individuals effectively hold the keys to the school. They determine if you get in and under what circumstances. Because this is the case, admissions deal with a high volume of parents and students daily. What you want to leverage out of these individuals is information. Getting the information from them will help you to not have to spend a lot of time with billing or the bursar's office.

The busiest times for these individuals are a few weeks before the semester starts. DO NOT wait until a week or two before classes start to contact admissions, student accounts, or any other office personnel. As I have stated before, these people receive a high volume of calls and questions the week or two leading up to the start of the semester and in order to get everyone taken care of in a timely manner, they usually will give cookie cutter, generalized information that may not fit your specific needs. You want to have all of the information that you need in terms of admissions and billing one month before classes begin at the latest. This goes for current college students as well because circumstances in your life may change causing you to have to pay for college an alternative way or see if you can earn a few credits at another school and transfer them over.

The first thing you want to do is do your own research. Looking on the school's website will help you to answer any general questions you may have, and it may bring up other questions that you may not have thought to ask in the first place. Remember, you want to use these people for information, so make their job easier by coming in with clear questions so that they can provide you with clear answers that tailor your needs. I implore you to write these questions down so that you won't forget something during the conversation.

Pro tip #3, if possible, go and speak to these people face to face. This way they can attach a face to a name and the conversation can be more personable. I am big on energy and how it is transferred. More things can get done in person rather than on the phone. In person, they may be able to provide you with print outs or other visuals that you otherwise would not have gotten through a phone conversation.

The Office of the Registrar, where admissions, financial aid, billing, and the rest of those individuals work act as the gatekeepers for your school. Respect their time and acknowledge their efforts and they will try and help provide you with anything that you may need within their power. These people cannot make everything happen, but no question should go unasked if you have it. Just make sure that you reach out to everyone at least a month before to not feel rushed and be clear about what you are asking or concerns that you may have.

Guidance Counselor/Academic Advisor

Last chapter, I touched on how your planner is your assistant. Well, it's time to add another member to your organization. In high school, you may have not had to use your guidance counselor at all, but in college it is a must.

Your guidance counselor or academic advisor will play as your management through college. They will consult with you about your classes and help keep you academically eligible throughout your college years. If you are an athlete, you pretty much won't have a choice and most likely will be assigned a specific athletic advisor because being a student athlete in college is a whole different ball game. If you are not an athlete, then be sure that your first year of college isn't your only year that you see your advisor. If you have a responsible advisor, being on the same page as them will give you so much peace of mind. On way too many occasions, I've witnessed students forgo their advisor meetings because they believed that they had all of the classes that they needed in order to meet their graduation requirements. A lot of times, this ends with the student being devastated because they have to wait another semester to graduate. Do not let this be you. Even if you feel like you have everything down and taken care of, you should still touch base with your advisor. This is a part of being an adult. One day in your career or your own business, you will have to attend meetings that you may not want to, but you must because communication is everything.

Getting insight from sources other than yourself is also valuable. Last chapter I harped on not taking electives that will be difficult for you. Your advisor will try to help you steer clear of these classes. The better relationship that you are able to build with your advisor, the better they will be able to cater to your learning style or class time preferences. I cannot stress to you enough how important this section of the book is. College can and will get a little overwhelming at some point, and this is why it is important to lean on as many resources and relationships that you can. I would not be working a 13-hour shift, then coming home to write this book if college was smooth sailing. I really want you to be more prepared for the valley's in college than I was. Meeting with my advisor once a semester took away so much worry for me. College comes with a fair amount of stress, with a great deal of it being things that are out of your control. The easier that you can make things that are in your control, the better you will be able to handle stress. Your office hours, your assistant (planner), and your management (guidance counselor), is your dream team that you should be leaning on. Use these resources effectively and as I have laid out and your college life academically speaking, will be on auto pilot.

Professors

Every professor is different. Their way of teaching, their grading styles, or even the way they respond to certain things. Yes, the same is true in high school and on down but the difference lies in the considerably larger amount of freedom that college professors have. Since this is the case, it is important to gage your professor's tendencies as early as possible in order to know what they will expect from you throughout the semester. Doing the bare minimum in one class may get you by, while it may piss off a professor in another.

Pro tip #4: never do the bare minimum when it comes to anything in life. You are not average. Carry yourself like the champion you are.

The longer you are in college the better you will be able to pick up on your professors' traits. You will get to the point where you will be able to tell how the semester will go by reading your professor's introductory email. We all have our own learning styles but inside the classroom, it will not always be so convenient for things to go your way as it pertains to how you are retaining information. One semester, I had a young lady in my class that would take notes on everything. She did great in that class because she would take the notes home and study them almost daily. This same woman was in another one of my classes that she actually struggled with initially. The professor breezed through all of his slides and never paused to give students time to jot down a note before giving out another piece of information. One day the woman was visibly frustrated at the professor for doing this and finally spoke up. The professor explained to the woman that she should focus more on listening and less time writing. The woman had to learn how to go without her notes but still thrive in the class. In class, give your professor whatever that they are looking for. Don't be too shy and not speak up in a talkative class and don't be too talkative in a class that requires a lot of listening. When you are done with your class time, then you will be able to go about your work however you like.

College professors are some of the brightest people that you will have access to in life. Yes you are in class for your credits, but this is also a time to pick the brains of your professors. These people study and teach for a living and trust me when I say that nothing gets them more excited than students asking genuine questions. These questions do not have to always be classroom related. I had a finance professor who I constantly asked about how the stock market works and when would be a good time for me to invest in it. The little small discussions that we had stuck with me even more so than the classroom lessons. Asking your professor questions is the best way to build a relationship with them. You can use this relationship to help open many doors for yourself. Interaction is a vital part of college that I am afraid is being lost, especially in smaller regional campuses. If you are in a bigger campus, you most likely are living amongst your peers and see your professors around campus often. If you are in a smaller school, things are much less intimate. Students in smaller campuses most likely live at home and have demanding work lives as well. This causes school to become just a pit stop in your day. This works for some, and you would not be in the wrong if you have this attitude toward school. The problem with this is that you keep yourself in a bubble and shut out very important opportunities that you could have obtained by having just a small sense of community. The saying "it's not about what you know, it's about who you know" is especially true in college. We are all learning the same things and getting the same degrees. The only things that will separate you from your peers are your grades (or "marks" shouts out to my readers across the pond) and your relationships that you leverage. Aim to have at least one small talk with each of your professors at least once during this semester. If you have nothing to ask them then simply ask them how their semester is going because trust me, professors don't get to hear this from students as much as they should. Go ahead and start building that relationship. You will thank me for it later.

Career Services

If you are looking to be employed after college, chances are the job that you want will require you to have some form of higher education. Unfortunately, having a degree is only the tip of the iceberg when it comes to competing for that new job. You have to be able to secure an interview. There are many ways to secure this interview but the two routes that college students mainly use are networking and resumes. Your ability to network and transfer your skills and background on to a piece of paper known as a resume effectively will directly affect your chance of getting a job that you want. Most colleges provide tools that will help you with these things but most students either don't know about these tools or do not care to use them. After reading this book, I want you to realize that doing the things that are only required of you in college is like entering into a raffle with only one ticket instead of maximizing your chances with five or six tickets. You must, you must, you must, be doing things outside of just going to classes to maximize your degree. Too many of us go or went to colleges wanting to know what that college could do for us. Do not place value into a school based on their name or prestige. Place value into the resources and opportunities that they offer that will allow you to maximize your degree and yourself in order to prepare you for the future. If you enjoy smaller class sizes because they allow you to be more successful, then don't lean towards a bigger school because of their big name. Some form of a career services department is essential to keeping you on the right track and will boost your chances of landing you in a favorable position after your college career comes to an end. As a freshman or sophomore, you won't have much interaction with career services yet. Your focus should be on working, interning, or volunteering at different places that will give you experiences that involve things such as teamwork, customer service, and leadership. If you are an athlete, it will be more difficult for you to do this but there will be more than enough resources out there that will help you find summer internships or other opportunities that will find you work. Some schools even have career fairs specifically for only student athletes. Your life after sports should always be a concern of yours when you are determining the school you are playing for.

During your junior year, you should be working on finding an internship or a job that will give you direct experience in whatever career you are trying to enter after school. Use your career center as a starting point when trying to obtain this opportunity. First make a resume (preferably not from a template) documenting your experiences with dates attached to them as well as any skills or interests you may have. If you are having trouble starting or have never done a resume before then do not worry! Someone in career services will be glad to help you with this. These people know what recruiters look for and will help you design your resume to be an extension of you. Even if you do know how to curate a resume, you should always run it by these professionals before you start using it to fish for opportunities. It would be foolish to make anything of importance to you and put it out without at least a second set of eyes looking at it. We all do things from only our perspective, and with this comes having blind spots that we aren't aware of. Having the career services team will help to give you a different perspective and fill holes that you may not have seen. There will also be different events throughout the year that will allow you to network and get a feel for what different careers have to offer. One of the biggest things that they do is put on a career fair/expo. Do not miss this, especially if you do not have anything yet lined up after college. Figure out the day of your career fair early and make sure you give yourself some time to attend it. The career center will provide you with a list of companies that will be there along with etiquette, advice, and ways to go about navigating the event. Since this is the College Blueprint I am going to tell you the only thing that you need to do to have a successful day at this career event.

Pro tip #5 is to get a list of what companies or opportunities that will be there. Circle the top three that you are interested in. You will do research on these places that will allow you to answer the questions: "why are you interested in us?" and "what would make you a good fit?." The goal is to be the first student at least one of these tables. They will be impressed with how you specifically stopped at their table first and have background knowledge on their company and what you could offer for them. To them, this means that you made them a priority so in turn, they will make it their priority to try to get you an interview, even if you do not have the strongest resume they have seen all day. Your interest that you show them and your professionalism that you display with doing your research before speaking to them, and your solid resume that you worked hard on should give you a great chance in landing at least one of those jobs in your top three.

Peers

Up to this point, college will come with some of the most amazing times in your life but also some of the most stressful. If you're reading this book and have already experienced some or all of college, you will understand that some of your closest friends that you've met from college came from being in difficult classes with each other or other stressful and annoying situations that you have found yourselves in. Being in college is a totally new situation that is unlike anything else. The best part about it, is that you won't be going through it alone. If you are going to work and school full time, guess what? Someone else is too. If you are away from home and missing your people, guess what? Someone else is too. Dealing with a difficult class with a difficult professor? Yup, someone else is dealing with that same class and professor as you. Tough times are made better when you have people around you who can empathize. Through empathizing with these people, bonds are built that will last you a lifetime. You will meet people in college that you will know for the rest of your life. Do not overlook the power of comradery.

Yes you are in school to receive a degree, but it does not end there. You are in college to experience and try new things but more importantly, meet people from different backgrounds, interact, and empathize with many different people. Good jobs understand that a degree is important not just because of the classes that you have to endure but because of the skills that it provides you with. There are few other places in the world where a Chinese woman can go down the hall and discuss calculus with a Nigerian man. You are exposed to so many different people that the average person won't be. Take advantage of this. I stress organization and structure because it allows you the free time to go out and hang with friends on the weekend. College is not one dimensional. It is not meant for your head to be buried in a book 24/7. After reading this book, it is my hope that you soak up all of the resources and the people that college has to offer. As long as you are a good person who helps and respects people, you will have no problem making friends in college. There is almost no bigger benefit in college than the people who you will meet. They will help you through hard times, they will provide you with opportunities, and most importantly they will teach you a lot about yourself and help you become a better person.

I will be short on this topic because I think that it is too important for me not to touch on. In college you will be doing a lot of growth and self-development. You won't be remotely the same person you are 4, 5, or 6 years from now. This makes dating in college very tricky. You will get to spend more time with your person of interest than you ever got to in high school and this can lead to a strong bond or attachment. Because we are constantly changing throughout our college years or late teens and early 20s in general (if you are an older student please stay with me because this applies to you too in some ways) it is important to give each other space and respect each other's growth. Growing means that you guys may eventually grow apart and that is completely ok because this whole thing is a learning experience. Learn from one another and more importantly HAVE FUN. Do not try to play house in college. You will have decades in life for that, afterward. Loving and getting to know yourself comes first, and if you aren't to the point of being confident in yourself or not knowing a lot about who you are, then you should consider being single until then. You don't want to find your identity in a relationship and become dependent on that relationship. Too many times I have seen major backslides happen after breakups in college. As long as you know and love yourself, things will stay grounded no matter what goes on in your relationship life.

Over time on your own, you will start to realize how important the relationships that you have with different people throughout college are. The earlier you develop these relationships, the stronger they will become. Always surround yourself with good people who cause you to push yourself through their words or actions. It is also important for you to become a valuable resource to other people as well. There are skills that you have as an individual that might help change someone's life. College provides access to more people in one place than you may ever have access to for the rest of your life. There is a small window to take advantage of this opportunity, so the faster you do this, the stronger your ties to these people become.

Chapter 4: Your Finances

There are countless books and videos that will teach you how to manage your finances in life. You will be hard pressed to not find some type of content that gives you information on how to handle money specific to the life you are living. For this reason, I am not going to play a financial advisor and give you strategies on how to do certain things as it pertains to the specifics, but I will give you two principles that I believe every college student besides the athletes should live by. Athletes' college lives are a lot different than the ones who don't play a sport but I will still throw you some tips.

Principle One: Income

Providing your time or service for money is how you obtain an income in order to take care of any payments or goals that you may have or buy things that you want. In our culture, being a college student is synonymous with being broke and in debt. With this book, I want to begin to help change this narrative. I want college students to start being seen as frugal and knowledgeable when it comes to money. It makes me very upset when I see the exploitation of students at times in higher learning, and I think as we become more aware of this, the more difficult it will be for loan companies or overpriced universities to exploit a student's strong want for a college degree. Notice that I said a student's "want" and not a student's need for a degree. We WANT to be doctors, lawyers, engineers, executives, or anything else that requires you to go to college, but we NEED to make a living. A living can be made without going to college and any person who isn't pro college will love to tell you that. The fact of the matter is, a college education is a tool that you use to enhance the wants that you have in your life. You don't have to become a doctor, lawyer, business professional, etc. to fulfill the needs in your life, but college is a tool that can help you fulfill those wants. Notice that I said "tool." College is not a magic wand that will suddenly grant you everything that you want.

The value of a college education lies in the resources and opportunities that it provides you and what you choose to do with it after you are finished. When you are done with college, you do not want to be burdened by high loan payments and mountains of debt. Ideally you want to be able to pay for most of your schooling but as most of us know, the world is not very ideal in most cases. The reality is, a lot of you have or will have to take out some loans for schooling, but the goal is to keep these loans at a minimum. A great rule of thumb to use when borrowing money for school is to take the average starting salary of whatever field you are looking to go in and try to never borrow any more than 30% of that. You want to ideally keep it at 20% or lower. If the starting salary of the profession that you want to go in is 50k a year, then you do not want to borrow more than 15k over your entire bachelorette program. If you have to borrow over 30% of that salary then you cannot afford that particular school at that time. This means that you should aim to pay for 70% or more of your tuition with grants, scholarships, or your own income. If you choose to live on campus, then note that you may have to borrow over 30%. Maintaining a proper income source is very important in college. In my eyes, working for income is just as much a part of college as taking classes are. Having a job not only gives you an income source to help pay for any expenses that you have, but it also teaches you how to actively budget and manage your money. Working also provides you with real world skills when it comes to interacting with the public and learning about leadership. Some students go their whole college careers without working and they are sometimes automatically thrown into a position of leadership that is hard for them to handle because they never had to deal with being scolded by angry customers or trying to manage a seemingly impossible load of work in a time crunch. The job(s) that you hold in college will boost your resume incredibly.

Working and going to school is hard work. If you follow the organization plan that I laid out for you, your schedule should take care of itself. This life can come with its issues, but money problems are something that you want to try to mitigate as much as possible in college. The recipe for this is finding work that pays over minimum wage, and money management. When I say find work that pays above minimum wage, I am not insinuating that minimum wage work or workers aren't valued. What I am insinuating, is that your time is very valuable because you have a limited amount of it. When you have limited time, the best thing that you can do is maximize that time in whatever it is that you are doing. Minimum wage is not maximizing your time. My first job was minimum wage in Indiana at a rate of $7.25/hr. I was saving my income for school and I began to realize simple math. It would obviously take me more time working here to save for my goal, than it would working somewhere else doing the same or similar work for $10/hr. In college, you will probably not have the time to supplement your life's expenses working hourly for your state's minimum amount. To some this may seem a little entitled especially if this is your first job. The fact of the matter is, you will be hard pressed to find jobs that still only pay minimum wage especially in a state like Indiana where the minimum wage rate is low. This is because employers recognize that their competition offers higher rates which results in lower turnover and a better-quality worker. Would you be more willing to go that extra mile for a job paying minimum wage, or a job that offers double that? Money is a measurement of value, and the price of something or the rate of something isn't what determines the value. YOU, as the consumer or the employee is what determines the value. In the case of creating an income for yourself while you are a full-time college student, think about the value that you place on your time.

When it comes to determining your value and ultimately your income this is the advice that I will give you. Work backwards. Your biggest expense as a college student is college. (If you are on scholarship, I recommend that you not skip this section because there will be nuggets in here for you guys as well.) Most colleges will allow you to pay in monthly increments, but some may not. In the case that you can arrange a monthly payment, this is the number you will want to start at when determining the income that you will need. It should go without saying that you should shop around different universities to determine who gives you the best value at the best rate. You also will want to work as many hours as you can during the summer. You may want to attend your state's big university, but the regional campus may offer you the same value for a price that you can afford. If the university that you choose does not offer monthly payments, then spend the summer working and putting as much down on your tuition as you can, then borrow the rest and just pay on your loan monthly. Remember that if you choose to borrow money towards your tuition, by the end of the year, you should be able to pay back around 70% of what you borrowed. In some cases, this rule of thumb eliminates a lot of possibilities of some of you going to a college you may have dreamed of going to because it is too expensive. This couldn't be further from the truth, you can borrow the money and go anyway and deal with the debt later, or you can go to a cheaper school for a year or two and work on saving and getting a scholarship and grant money to go to that dream school. The first choice may seem good enough for some, and by all means if you have parents or guardians who are able to cosign those loans and be tied to your debt for some years then have a ball, but if this is not an option for you, then the second choice will be the way to go. It is a lot easier telling your parents who didn't cosign any loans for you that you may want to switch your major than explaining this to parents who have thousands of dollars of debt attached to their names. I have seen many students who have taken out a large amount of loans that their parents have underwritten, be afraid to tell them that they want to change their major for one reason or another. This usually results in the student not changing their major and performing poorly in their classes, which then usually results in academic probation. If you want to avoid the possibility of this stress, try to never overpay or over borrow for college. Not borrowing over 30% of your projected income is a good benchmark and I understand that sometimes this isn't possible. It is important to just always use your best judgement, and always use some of your income to pay for schooling.

The next thing you want to look at before determining the income that you want to have, is looking at your monthly bill and food budget. There may not be a lot of wiggle room here, so it is important to be honest with yourself. What are some things that can be cut out? Do you pay for a monthly gym membership when you can workout at your school's gym for free? Are you eating out more than you are cooking on a weekly basis? (This should almost never be the case as a college student) Look at your budget and determine where you can trim the fat of the things that can be substituted for cheaper options or just eliminated completely. I may sound preachy, but I want you to have the freedom to eventually do the things that you really want. In college, creating memories and bonds are very important. You don't want to be the one to miss out on that big concert or that weekend brunch with friends because you weren't tight and efficient with your budget during the month. Remember that freedom is a by-product of discipline.

The next number you want to look at is your emergency fund/savings. If you drive in college, your car can and will betray you. You should put some money aside for this reason alone. Too many times have I seen car troubles plague a student's life for a period of time. You want to be prepared for things like this. It is a lot harder to study for that bio exam when you are worried about who will be able to give you a ride to and from work the next day. Make sure your car is always properly maintained and address problems as quickly as possible. Do not be afraid to ask your parents for help at times. Most parents will be proud to see that you are budgeting and being independent and will be more than proud to help you out as best as they can when it comes to the unexpected troubles in life. The last expense you want to take into account when determining your income is your fun/entertainment expense. As a responsible college student, the more deliberate you are about your weekend or your free time expenses,

the better college experience you will have. You are
doing yourself a disservice when money leaks out of
your bank account that wasn't accounted for in your
weekly budget and then your friends want to do
something fun that you can't afford to do. When I say
be intentional about this expense, I mean to not treat
this expense as money left over after you are done
taking care of the higher priority expenses. Even
though fun and entertainment aren't the highest on
your priority list, your joy and happiness is still a
priority. Throughout college, my friends meant the
world to me and there were things that I was able to
do with them and memories that I was able to create
because during the week or month, I simply made
better choices to save me money to do the things that
brought me joy. Once again, college can and will be
stressful at times. Taking care of your mental,
physical, and emotional well-being is imperative to
combat any kind of stress in your life during or even
after college is over. Your fun/entertainment expense,
or what I like to call your Freedom Fund, goes into
aiding your self-care. Be as intentional about this

expense as everything else, even though it comes last on the list.

   After you have your monthly tuition, bills/food, savings, and freedom fund expenses all calculated, this number will help aid you in determining the income you want to seek out. Earlier in the chapter, I explained how important it is to be honest with your budget. It is not likely that you will have a job while in school that is paying you 5k a month after taxes to fund your life. Be real with yourself. You may have to live at home at first (which I highly recommend if you attend college locally). You may have to find a school with a price point more suitable for you but also offers you a quality education. Having an income that helps you meet your monthly expenses is a good way to determine your value when job hunting. Always be looking for ways to increase your income and while keeping your expenses as low as possible while in school. While this is important, it is also important that you not drop out of school in order to earn more money. Once classes start to become tougher usually around the second semester of your sophomore year, I have seen students become more interested in working more hours at working and begin to neglect school until they finally drop out. Remember, do not take your eyes off of the prize, which is that degree you will use as a tool to help you do the things you really want in life and possibly make even more money.

Principle Two: C's may get degrees, But A's get you Paid

Has someone ever told you that grades don't matter in college as long as you are passing? Well in theory this is true because with a low GPA, you will walk across the same stage and earn the same degree as someone with a 4.0 GPA. There is one difference that I might add, and that is by not getting the best grades possible, you are leaving money on the table. If you are a high schooler reading this right now, your grades not only will get you accepted into the college you want but they will also pay you if they are good enough. Grades are not the only thing that can get you scholarships of course but it is the most basic way. If you are a student, you have to be in class anyway, so why not just use the tools that I laid out for you, or whatever works to get the grades in order to maximize the benefits that you can get out of school. Also, the accolades that you receive from your grades will aid in helping you eventually land that dream job. If a company sees that you are balancing having a job and getting exemplary grades while in college, this will tell them a lot about you and your work ethic. There are a lot more upsides for keeping great grades than there are with having mediocre grades. There is a limited amount of time that you will have in college, and it is key to maximize this time as much as possible, by doing things that will benefit you in the long run. I am a big believer in cause and effect. Some of my friends may think that some of my cause and effect examples are a little out there, but I understand that your life is one big chain reaction. Here is an example of one of my "out there" cause and effect examples. If you choose to excel in your academics, there will be many scholarship opportunities available to you. After you graduate, you will have low debt and be able to save more money and have a higher credit score, allowing you to put a bigger down payment on a house therefore obtaining a lower interest rate and ultimately owning and paying off a house a lot quicker than you would be able to if you didn't take care of your grades in college. Getting that high GPA can literally kick start your life and allow you to build wealth and avoid being trapped in a hamster wheel for the rest of your life. One of the reasons that I am writing this book is because I want you guys to take college seriously. If done right, college can be a tool that you use to propel your life forward in a way that you can't even imagine. If handled poorly, college can saddle you with a mountain of debt, cause stress and anxiety, and feel like an anchor instead of wings. It is time to stop looking at college as THE answer to a better life. You and your decisions are the keys to that better life and college is merely a tool (a hell of a tool) that you will use to help you get there. Your decision making and work ethic will determine your true value after you graduate, not just the big bold name at the top of your degree.

Managing your finances will be a part of your life for maybe as long as you live. The information that you learned from the principles that I have shared in this chapter does not stop here. Always be doing your own research and learn new ways to go about managing your money. There is not one right way to do this but as long as more money is coming in than going out, then you are on the right track. Some of you have dreams of going to certain universities that might not make sense in terms of your financials right now. This does not mean that your dream university is no longer an option. You have to make a clear-cut plan on how you will eventually get to the university that you want. A lot of students use community college as a way to aid in getting them into the university that they really want. Some students start out at their local university with plans of doing this but end up just staying where they are after they realize that their local university provides them with the same resources at a more affordable price. We are all adults or becoming adults, and in becoming responsible men and women, it is important to think about the present, but it is imperative to think about your future. Doing this will require temporary sacrifice and foregoing some things that may cause you happiness in the moment but hinder you in the future. Student loan companies are in the business of appealing to your youth and your need for that feeling of immediate gratification. Because of this, they sometimes offer these large loans with high interest rates that will allow you to go to that dream university. Do not fall for this. Make the sound decision of creating your own income and using that to help pay your way into school so that you will be able to go to that dream college for free on scholarship.

Chapter 5: Your Major

What do you major in? If you are currently in college, you have probably heard this question already more times than you can count. It's almost like your major is part of your identity while in school. Why is this the case? Well, in most cases college is a means to an end. Your end being whatever career or grad school program you intend on going into after you graduate. Because of this, people can get a glimpse into who you are, or your interests based off of the major that you choose to be in. For a lot of new students, this is not the case. These students are undecided on their major and not quite sure what they should study. The first year in college usually focuses on general education classes to help guide new students into their respective major. While these classes are important, I believe that more thought should go into choosing your major than just the type of classes that you like or don't like to take. For example: I knew that after I graduated, I wanted to be in a position of leadership or management.

There wasn't a specific thing that I wanted to manage but I just knew that I could see myself in that type of role so going into business management was a no brainer for me. I didn't take into account the marketing, accounting, or finance classes that I would have to take, I just focused on the role that I wanted to have when I was finished with schooling.

Determining the role that you want to play after college may spook some students out. Committing to a major for two-plus years can be a little nerve wracking especially when there is a lot of money and time tied into this decision. Our world is constantly changing and so are our decisions, so how could we expect to land on one solid choice when it comes to this? My advice to you would be to keep your thoughts broad. I said that I wanted to be in a position of leadership. This did not include leadership for a specific company or leadership of a specific kind. I just wanted to lead. Being a leader is in the fabric and foundation of my being. When you are remodeling a house, the foundation is usually always the same no matter what changes in the house. Even if your decision changes with who you want to be, it will rarely change when it comes to who you are and what you want to do. For those of you who know exactly what you want to do after college and have your major figured out, ask yourself this question. "Why do I want to be a (insert career)?" Some of you are in Nursing to become a physician's office nurse because you want to make a difference or help people. Some of you are in criminology to be a criminal investigator for the same reasons.

Throughout your time in college you may wake up and realize that being a physician's office nurse or a criminal investigator is totally not what you want to do. This may well be the case, but there is a small chance that you will no longer want to help people or make a difference and there are still opportunities to do that with a nursing or criminology degree.

Keeping this in the back of your mind makes picking a major a lot less anxiety inducing. In the first chapter of this book, I talked about having a why. Yes college is important but jumping into it without thought leads to a high probability in dropping out. Learning who you are and what lights your soul on fire is a part of determining your "Why" in college. Math was not very fun for me, but I knew to get to where I wanted to go, calculus had to be dealt with. If I went into college with no purpose or just because my mom or Michelle Obama told me to, I probably would not have gotten through calculus or managerial accounting. Having your why creates your purpose and your purpose creates a will to go through any obstacle put in front of you. Do you think every doctor in the world right now loved going to chemistry or biology class? Most likely not, but they knew that they had to bite that bullet. When thinking of a major to possibly go into, think of what you want to do first. Do you want to lead, do you want to help people, do you want to create, do you see yourself bringing joy to others? If you are struggling with deciding your major or struggling in your current major, ask yourself those questions first. I wanted to lead. Surgeons can be leaders, but I pass out at the site of blood. That eliminated about four majors for me right there. Do not think that you are being boxed in when you choose a major, instead think of your major as something that is helping to guide you towards your purpose.

If you are already set on exactly what you want to do after college, then consider yourself very fortunate. My advice to you would be to keep your options open but keep going hard for what you want. I am currently writing this book in the spring of 2020. Right now, we are in the middle of a national pandemic. This is a rare occurrence but right now it is our reality. A lot of people are out of work right now due to so many businesses being shut down. This pandemic will eventually pass but it will change how some businesses are done moving forward. Your job could be affected from something like a pandemic at any time, so it is important to have other interests and skills to be able to continue conforming with the economy. Education is not college exclusive. Always be learning new skills and ways to supplement your life. The more information you learn and skills you obtain, the more valuable you will be to the market. We will always need individuals in things like healthcare, transportation, and law enforcement. Begin to think about skills that you can inherit for industries that are essential so that you will always be of value to the marketplace. For example, I am in management and I was a supervisor for a trucking company that laid me off. This same company needs truck drivers to transport more goods during this pandemic so it would behoove me to get my CDL (commercial driver's license) the next time around.

Are you on your last straw and definitely want to change your major? Changing your major is a very serious decision that in most cases will cost you a significant amount of time. A lot of people, including me, did not graduate in 4 years. I was a transfer student, so I had to change my plan of study. I was still in business school so there was not a huge change, but for some people this is not the case. Students wanting to switch from economics to accounting will have an easier time than someone switching from communications to Nursing. If you are thinking about changing your major, first try looking into whatever program you are in and see if you would be interested in a different plan of study. For example, if you are in business economics and want to switch majors, it would behoove you to look within the business school for something else you may be interested in. Doing this limits the number of classes that won't be used towards your degree. If you want to change from business school to another program like humanities or engineering, there are some classes that you took and paid for that won't go toward your new major. I don't want to call it wasted time, but it is definitely money out the window. This is the reason why some students are frightened to choose a major in the first place. As long as you know who you are and what you want to accomplish in your life, you will be able to let that guide you towards an appropriate major. The degree that you receive from your major will unlock so many doors for you that you can't even imagine. Don't get caught up into a specific job that you may go on to do after college. Think about your purpose and use the opportunity or the job to fulfil that purpose. You may have to take a few classes that you loathe but use this book to help you get through those classes and go towards your destiny. This is why I believe in this book so much. Those of us who have graduated understand significance in things that current students tend to look over, and the insignificance of the things that a lot of students look too deeply into. Plan ahead, write things down, use your resources to mitigate stress, work hard, have fun, manage your finances or your finances will definitely manage you, get sleep, stay hydrated, and most importantly, believe in yourself. Without the belief in yourself, the will to win through adversity will not be there. You often hear about believing in yourself even if the naysayers don't. The naysayers are usually not why some students begin to doubt themselves. It is instead the people in your lives that were there for you and believed in most things that you have done and the people who you look at for stability and comfort that will eventually lose their belief in you once you take a step outside of that box. They will not lose their belief in you out of malice or ill will. They do it because they love you and want to limit the amount of risks that you take that could end in pain or disappointment. This will not happen to everyone, but for some of you, this will be a very real reality. When you are ready to stand on what you believe in on your own, your mind will start to become unbreakable, because even if you fail, you will eventually land wherever you are supposed to be. There are future hall of fame coaches out there who had dreams of going pro, and even though some people didn't believe in them and they ultimately didn't make it to that level, they ended up coaching pros. "Shoot for the moon, because even if you fail, you will land amongst the stars." Believe in yourself, know yourself, choose that major, and let that be the key to get you into the door of unlimited opportunities.

Chapter 6: Your Stress Management

When it comes to stress, there are usually three ways that students deal with it. It is important to recognize which category that you fall into. The first way is to run from it. Running from stress is a lot of the time a coping mechanism for some individuals. Stressful situations can cause anxiety or trigger people in ways that can be very severe. People like this are very good at removing themselves from stress inducing situations and environments. These individuals also tend to avoid confrontational events and either go with the flow or distance themselves.

The second way some students deal with stress is to work through it. Stress might affect people like this or sometimes or it may not but either way, their response will be the same. These individuals can usually thrive in most situations and are a huge asset to any business or company. The biggest problem with this way of coping with stress is that these people are usually over worked by themselves or their companies and they can begin to abandon other areas in their lives such as relationships, self-care, and other things in order to have the capacity to deal with that which causes the most stress.

The third way that some students deal with stress is to mitigate it. Mitigating stress takes equally from the first and second examples. Sometimes these individuals run from the stress, other times they deal with it head on. These students will pick their battles which in a lot of cases can be a good thing. The only problem with mitigating and limiting stress in your life is that after a while you will start to become weak at dealing with important stress that makes you uncomfortable and would rather deal with the unimportant option because it is more appealing. For example, some students who like to mitigate stress would rather have the stress of waiting to cram at the last minute to study for a final, than the stress of taking out the time to study for the final in advance. The latter option is probably the way to go but if someone is used to cramming, and this gets them by, then they could get stuck in their ways and it could be difficult for them to take things to the next level.

There are pros and cons to each of the three examples but before I delve further into those, it is important to first understand stress. The definition of stress is "a state of mental or emotional strain or tension resulting from adverse or very demanding circumstances." The thing that stands out to me the most are the words mental and emotional. Back when I used to play basketball and my mom would see me begin to get tired, she would yell "It's 80% mental and 20% physical". Back then, I would always scoff at that notion because she wasn't the one sprinting up and down the court at the time draining energy. It wasn't until I was a senior in high school that I began to understand her concept. I was a transfer student coming from Indianapolis to Kennesaw, GA. It was bittersweet for me because I had to move from my hometown and wouldn't be able to graduate with people that I went to school with since elementary but it was sweet because I was in a new environment and I was finally going to be able to go to college in a year's time. I went to a small private school named North Cobb Christian. NCC is a tight knit blue-collar K-12 private school that was a whole new world to me. I previously came from Lawrence North which was a large public high school in Indianapolis. During my senior year at NCC I ran into a lot of bumps at first and wanted to just leave there and attend North Cobb High School which was the more familiar big public school 2.5 miles down the road. My mentor, coach Walter Jordan, explained to me that even though I could not see it, I was in a great position at a great school that will put me at a greater advantage to succeed after high school. I was hesitant, but just like hundreds of young men and women around the Atlanta, GA area, I trusted him.

Eventually I began to adapt and take pride in my small school. I ended up not only gaining a great deal of respect for my teammates but for the student body as a whole. In Indianapolis, I also played some varsity basketball but in Georgia it was different. In Indy it felt like I was just playing for the team. In Georgia it felt like I was playing for the team, the students, the faculty, hell the whole K-12 school. During the season we eventually ran into the big public school down the road, North Cobb. Historically, North Cobb Christian did not play this school often due to being in different leagues and more obviously the size difference of the schools. My senior class graduated a little over 60 students while North Cobb graduated close to, if not 500 seniors. Their basketball team was GOOD. A few of them were on my AAU team during the summer so I kind of knew what they had to offer. All five of their starters were seniors who in the previous year, made it to the final 4 in the state's highest class. These guys were favored to win state this year and we were a small threat to them. Three out of the five of our starters, including me, were transfer students. We all had a chip on our shoulder and something to prove not only to ourselves, but to the state as well. It was not just the team with this chip on our shoulders, but the whole school had it. We felt looked over and counted out. We were out for blood. The game ended up being in our small cramped gym full of familiar faces but even more full of the opposing teams' fans. There were feelings of uncertainty, angst, and stress, but as soon as that ball tipped, those feelings began to fade, and we started playing our game. We came out of the gates hard and took an early lead. They eventually started to pull closer but by then we were too much into a rhythm and overwhelmed them. Our smaller crowd overwhelmed theirs, and our coaches overwhelmed theirs as well. We ended up winning by nearly 20 points and even though I played almost every minute of it, I felt like I could keep going. It was then that I finally understood my mom shouting "80% mental and 20% physical" was about. I wanted to win for my school so badly, that I wasn't focused on running up and down the court, I wasn't focused on the stress of playing such a good team or being tired. I was purely focused on winning. In that moment, from a high school basketball game I realized how powerful the mind is. Earlier we defined stress as being "a state of mental or emotional strain or tension resulting from adverse or very demanding circumstances." Stress is real ladies and gentlemen.

But realize that it is just a state of MENTAL or EMOTIONAL strain. I love sports because they often imitate life. Life is also 80% mental and the rest is up to your physical ability to actually do it once you put your mind to it. This brings me to two types of stress which are necessary stress and unnecessary stress.

Have you ever heard the term "pressure makes diamonds"? This term is often used when someone is in a stressful or pressurized situation that will end up benefiting them once they get through it. This is a perfect example of necessary stress. In terms of being a student, your journey to success will come with forms of necessary stress. The key is to limit the amount of unnecessary stress as much as possible. Following the principles that I have laid out in this easy read; will definitely help you avoid a lot of unnecessary stress. Unnecessary stress is anything or even anyone that takes away from your success or joy the more time that you spend on it, or them. I will share with you an example. The more you study the better off you will be during your exam but the more time you spend worrying about your exam, the less time you are left with to prepare for the inevitable exam.

Pro tip #6, worrying without action when it comes to school is almost always unnecessary stress. Sometimes you will study or prepare yourself as much as possible and you will still worry, but your preparation will usually take care of you and the more experienced you become as a student, the less worries you will start to have because you will be more confident in your style of preparation.

It is important to start recognizing the stress in your life that is necessary and unnecessary. I promise you that doing this will take you so far and cut out unneeded worry and drama. Each of us have different things that will trigger our stress. The first thing that I recommend you do is figuring out the source of this stress and then how you will address it.

In the beginning of this chapter, I went through three ways that people address stress. They run from it, mitigate it, or work through it. When it comes to unnecessary stress, working through it is the worst choice. As previously stated, stress is a mental thing. When you begin to entertain unnecessary stress constantly by working through it, you will begin to condition your mind to adapt to unnecessary stress this way. This will mean that you will start to become comfortable wasting your time on unnecessary stress and form bad habits. The type of students who do this usually have a hard time getting through college. College is presented to you in a way that is unstructured. In high school, everyone has their classes at the same times and on the same days for the most part. This makes things like group work easier because almost everyone will be free after school is out. In college there is no such thing as "after school is out." I had some classes that went until p.m. some semesters. It will be your job to structure your weeks on your own. This means that as a student, your time is limited and valuable. The more time you spend on unnecessary stress, the less time you will have to do valuable things and the more you will struggle. This pertains to life outside of being a student too. There may be times where you will have to work through this negative stress but understand the kind of stress it is and discover ways to avoid it the next time it comes into your life. This is now where mitigating the unnecessary stress comes into place. The better you are at recognizing this type of stress, the more often you will be able to sidestep it. I took a calculus class where the exam questions were way longer and more difficult than the homework questions that we had been assigned throughout the week. During the first exam, I caused myself a lot of unnecessary stress by worrying and clouding my head with negative thoughts. I knew that these exams were probably going to be this way going forward, so I went to the tutoring center to do my homework but afterwards I would do the difficult problems at the end of the chapter that weren't assigned and receive help with them from any available tutor. At the time it was very tedious and stressful doing this extra work, but it resulted in me receiving as on the next few exams. I substituted stressing out unnecessarily with the good stress of preparing for these exams in a different but more tedious way. Not changing anything and always stressing out about how hard the next exam would be would not have benefited me. Do not try and accept stress that you have the ability to mitigate. As a young man, I have found success that I never could have imagined by doing this.

The last option I want to talk about when it comes to unnecessary stress is running from it. For most students, group work will be a huge part of your college career. Some like it, most don't, but the reality is that you will come across it and it does serve a purpose. An example of running away from unnecessary stress is avoiding working with the kid who is always late or unengaged in class. The key to running from something is recognizing it first. I couldn't run from that first calculus exam but if I knew the content on it beforehand, I would have been able to run from the issue and act on it quicker. This being said, even though you may do a good job by running from the stress that you deem unnecessary, there still may have to be times that you address the issue to make them disappear. Running from bad stress does not mean that you are ignoring it.

Sometimes the best way to run from it is by responding swiftly. These situations don't happen often but when they do, it can become really annoying if not addressed properly. Sounds confusing? Allow me to explain. You may one day have a coworker who is on a health kick, so he heats up fish every day in the break room. You find the fishy smell to be repulsive, but you are smart, so you don't allow yourself to be stressed out, you just run from the problem by eating in your car. The issue with this is, the problem still exists. You are just using a variable, which in this case is your car to act as a buffer between you and your problem. One day, your car may have to be in the shop overnight and you need a ride to work. This time, you don't have that buffer to help you out. If you would have talked to your coworker about your concern, or a manager to help you or him find a new place to eat, then this would have been taken care of in the event that your car was not available. This goes for my group work example as well. Your professor may end up actually pairing you with the kid that is unengaged. You still have a way to avoid the problem by assigning his work to him ahead of time so he knows what he will be held accountable for. These are ways that you can recognize a problem and quickly and eliminate them. These explain running from the stress by first running to fix the problem.

To recap ways to deal with unnecessary stress:

1. Avoid it if you can identify it beforehand by dodging it or addressing it.
2. If you cannot avoid it initially, learn ways that you can begin to mitigate it.
3. Never accept it because accepting unnecessary stress will become a huge time-wasting black hole in your collegiate career. Your brain will learn how to cope with bad stress.

Finding a style to handle necessary stress is based more on the individual and how they respond to certain levels of stress. There can be such a thing as too much necessary stress but that strictly depends on the individual. No matter what anyone tells you, college is different from high school. This doesn't mean that it is easier or more difficult, but the dynamics are definitely different. You must learn how much stress that you are able to take on early and plan around it. Some of you will not be able to have a two- or three-hour study session so you may have to block out smaller time periods. The best way to determine your threshold for necessary or positive stress, is to simply stick to your planner aka your "assistant" and begin to adjust things so that it works just right for you. Some things you will have to mitigate and other things you will be able to work through. This is why handling positive stress is so different from person to person. Once you have your mind in the right place to actually do this, your life and experience in college will open up and afford so many opportunities to you.

Running away from necessary stress is sometimes okay but should never be done more than sparingly and will create bad habits if you continue to run. The bigger the responsibility or necessary stress that you are taking on, the more you should think about mitigating it and not just working through it if you believe that you are about to run from it or avoid it. For example, if you find yourself in a situation where you have a short amount of time to study because you may have not managed your time well, but you are tired and would rather just sleep and take your chances on the exam, you want to first determine if there is a way that you can get at least a small amount of studying in. Since stress is so mental, defeat starts in the mind. Once you determine that it's too late and you don't want to study, then your action follows. The key is using your mind to unlock or trick your actions into doing what's right. If you begin to break your studying down into 10-minute increments, you may be able to push yourself longer than what you may have thought. Once upon a time I was in this same spot. I was dead tired and simply did not want to get up and grab my backpack, take out my books and laptop to study. I told myself that I would give it at least 10 minutes just to look over some things. Once I started to actually work, 10 minutes flew by, so I gave myself another 10. I figured that since I already was up and working, what sense would it make for me to just put everything up after only 10 minutes. I ended up studying an extra 40 minutes all because I was able to use my mind and my reasoning to trick myself into working longer. 80% mental....20% physical.

Some days you are going to be at your limit and just not want to deal with a specific task. We all have or will have those days where our mental capacity for taking on any kind of stress let alone positive stress is just impossible. In your chapter in this book on organization, I touched on the importance of structuring your days so that you will have more dedicated free time. What free time does is rejuvenate your mind and body so that you will be able to take on your business and duties more efficiently. If you do not take care of your mind and body, they will begin to fail you and cause you to constantly run from life's necessary stress. Things like anxiety, depression, or mental health troubles could also be things that drain your mental capacity. If you feel like these are issues, speak to your academic advisor, or another representative of your school and to figure out options that are available to you to help combat these things. Universities understand that college is a new experience and having free counseling available to students in order to help propel them into a position of success is very important. Protecting and constantly working on your mental well-being will cover you so much in college.

Breathing and blinking are two of the very few lists of things you are able to do consistently without thinking. Everything else requires your mind to activate first and then your actions to follow. Your mind can create good habits for you, or it can create bad habits. Take care of yourself and yourself will take care of you when it comes to tackling your necessary stress.

Congratulations, you made it to the end of a very important chapter. The first chapter in this book is titled "Your Why." In it, I explained that having a "why" is important because it gives you reason and motivation to keep going through the stress and tough times. I believe that stress is something that for a long time, wasn't a big topic in schools across the nation but is now becoming more and more of a priority. Creating balance in your life is super important when it comes to dealing with stress. Things like having and following a planner, exercising, resting, putting the right foods in your body are things that your mind and body loves. Your mind especially loves doing what it wants to do from time to time and that is completely ok. It is important to listen to your mind every once in a while in order to keep your sanity. Have that ice cream this weekend, get some extra studying out the way so you can hang out with your friends at that new bar on Friday. The more disciplined you are with taking care of yourself and your responsibilities, the more often you will be able to indulge in the things that you sometimes crave. I want each of you who are attending college that are reading this book to have the best time possible, but you have to work and you have to take care of yourself because you will end up burnt out or running from the stress that is necessary for you to handle your responsibilities. There is no way around this. Get a planner, follow that planner, rest, put the right things in your body, and then always HAVE FUN.

Chapter 7: My Thank You

Guys from the bottom of my heart, I want to thank you guys for taking out the time to read this book. I wrote it with the sole purpose of helping others get a little further ahead, a little sooner than I did. There is no one right way to do college but there are definitely multiple wrong ways. With this information, you are now equipped with general principles that will allow you to not even come close to those wrong ways. I ended up dropping out of college twice. The first time was because I didn't have a "why" so I began to become burned out and lost the will to finish the semester. The second time I didn't want to be out of school, but my finances were not in order. Your "why" and your "finances" are two things that were touched on in this book and everything else that I touched on were also things that I once failed at. I'm able to tell you about unnecessary stress because at one point I consumed myself with it. I'm able to tell you about planning and organization because there was a point in my life where things were disorganized. Every single thing you have read about in this book are lessons that I had to learn and things that I had to adapt to. I eventually became a successful student who went on to graduate but not before running into very real bumps that almost derailed me from accomplishing my goals. You too will run into real problems, but it is my hope that with the lessons covered in this book there will be a few less bumps and learning curves you will have to deal with.

Life is a journey. You will not be able to dictate every turn of this journey. Some of you will find yourself outside of school due to circumstances beyond your control. One of the differences in life between those who reach their goals and those who don't, is the ability to not accept your circumstances. Overtime, life's problems can begin to pile up if not addressed properly. Before I went off to college during my freshman year, I was having issues with my mom. Our relationship wasn't in the best place, but I thought going far away to college would fix things. That was unaddressed problem #1. I felt that my mental health was starting to decline but I just looked at it as me being weak. That was problem #2. My grandfather who lived back in Indiana used to give me a call every weekend (I was attending the beautiful Radford University in the hills of southwest Virginia at the time). It was good hearing from him every weekend and I was beginning to form a great relationship with him because we never really lived close enough to each other. During the second semester, because I didn't address problem #2 I started to fall into depression. I even stopped answering calls from my grandfather for a couple of weeks because I just had it in my mind that I would get back to him. A short time after this, I had to fly up to Indiana because I found out that he was dying of stage 4 cancer. I'm glad I got to see him before he passed away but in the last voicemail that he sent me after I didn't answer he said that he wanted to talk to me about something. I was angry that I didn't get to have that last conversation with him, and his death became problem #3. I didn't take time to grieve, I just jumped right back into school and basketball. These three problems that I did not address set me back a bit. Even though this was the case, I did not let my circumstance consume me. I knew that I had to get out of Virginia to put myself in a different state of mind, but I couldn't go back home because my mother and I were at odds. I ended up going up to live with my aunt and uncle in Hammond, IN. I had no money, friends, job, or way to get back into school and I could have easily just used my position in life as an excuse not to win but I didn't because I followed my "why." My journey took many unexpected turns, but I never lost sight of the destination. Most of you guys will experience some pain and disappointment in your journey and that's ok because there will always be an opportunity to grow through that. The important thing is to not give into the pain and disappointment and eventually reach success despite bumps that you run into. I have been fortunate enough to see people who have juggled parenthood, dealt with the death of a loved one, struggle with anxiety, come from poverty, or even return to college after 20+ years and graduate and eventually go on to live the life that they dreamed of. Guys there are very few problems under the sun that you will face that will keep you from getting that degree. Without the pain and adversity in my life, I would not have been able to convey this book full of information to you.

"Go confidently in the direction of your dreams! Live the life you've imagined. As you simplify your life, the laws of the universe will be simpler." - Henry David Thoreau.

This is your life. Take advantage of every moment, opportunity, and resource available to you. I hope that I have been able to simplify your lives in college in some way so that the universe may open up to you and grant endless possibilities. Once again, thank you for taking the time out to read this book. Whether you're a current, new, or experienced student, or just a curious individual, I've kept you in mind throughout this entire process. I hope that I inspired you guys to share information with those who are with you and those who will come after you.

Continue to better yourself and remember to always
go confidently in the direction of your dreams!

Peace.

Acknowledgements

First and foremost, I obviously have to thank God. Even in my times of doubt and disobedience, you have made yourself clear to me more times than I deserve. I want to thank the matriarch of our family, my grandmother Mary Hartley. The kindest and most unselfish, yet fiercest woman I know. Granny you are the very definition of a strong black queen. Next I want to thank my Uncle Kyle and my Aunt Robin. When I left Radford, they took me in without hesitation. They also taught me indirectly how to move in a marriage and I hope to one day model that with my future spouse. Without you guys, graduating from PNW would not have been possible so thank you. I want to thank the following people who were there through my college journey that helped shape me into the man I am today and the even greater man that I hope to become: LaLa Hartley, Uncle Randall Saulesbury, Uncle Bryant Hartley,Uncle Darrin Smith, all of my managers who gave me chances so I could beef up my resume and keep cash in my pocket,

Bri Lopez, Amara Natal, Janessa Salinas, my Radford coaches and teammates, as well as Purdue Northwest university as a whole. There are more people that I am missing, just know that I am beyond thankful. I want to thank my stepmother Shun for being there for me and teaching me the importance of quality time with family. I want to thank my dad Hulian Terrell III for putting things in perspective for me as an adult. Thank you for the lessons that you have provided me with that I will carry for life. Thank you to my little sister London Riley Terrell, for always putting a smile on my face. I love you and I cannot wait to continue seeing you grow up into a beautiful and intelligent young lady. Thank you to Coach Walter Jordan. Coach Jordan has many accolades in his life. Indiana basketball hall of famer, Indiana State champion, Purdue basketball star, NBA player, coach, you name it. Though all of these sports accomplishments are great, Walter Jordan is a Hall of Fame human being that has helped change and shape countless lives. Your positive attitude is contagious, and your ability to connect with the youth is unparalleled. Coach Jordan, I challenge you to write an autobiography because I know that your story will inspire and motivate others to be a pillar in their community just like yourself.

I want to thank my stepfather Emmanuel Thompson for teaching me hard work and how to provide for loved ones. Thank you to my sister, also my day 1 Janasia Thompson. Growing up, we laughed, we cried, we fought, and we lived together. We may have not lived near each other for some years, but I feel your energy every day. In times of weakness I hear your voice inside my head saying, "You got this bro." Your will to do things your way, even if that means rebelling from time to time inspires me because you always come out satisfied with yourself. I love you and will always have your back. Last but not least I want to thank my best friend, my guide, my light, at times my nemesis, my mom Katrina Hartley-Thompson. Thank you for giving birth to me, thank you for always putting me first, and thank you for instilling in me lessons in which some I did not understand at the time, but eventually they became crystal clear as an adult. Growing up I was a momma's boy and we were inseparable. As I became older, we started not to see eye to eye on some things. The older I become; I realize that this is ok. You raised me to be smart, independent, strong, and resilient. Any success that has ever come my way as an adult is attributed to the boy you raised to become the man I am today. Thank you, I love you, and there is no way I could ever repay you except by living my life to the fullest and representing you by contributing to my family, my community, and my dreams every day.

Made in the USA
Columbia, SC
14 October 2023

24466978R00069